Contents

P9-EES-674

*"My object was
to present some of the great truths
concerning man's spiritual life
in simple language;
treating it,
not as an intense form of other-worldliness
remote from the common ways
and incompatible with the common life,
but rather as the heart of religion
and therefore of vital concern to ordinary
men and women."*

EVELYN UNDERHILL

30 Days with a Great Spiritual Teacher

Grace through Simplicity

■ ■ ■ ■ ■ ■ ■ ■ ■ ■ ■ ■ ■

The Practical Spirituality of

EVELYN UNDERHILL

JOHN KIRVAN

ave maria press AmP **Notre Dame, Indiana**

JOHN KIRVAN, who conceived this series and has authored most of its titles, writes primarily about classical spirituality. Other recent books include *God Hunger, Silent Hope, Raw Faith,* and *There is a God, There is No God.*

The thirty meditations that comprise the heart of this book are based on the writings of Evelyn Underhill. They have been freely adapted from *Practical Mysticism*, an early work of the twentieth-century English mystic and spiritual director, and from her masterpiece, *Mysticism*. Her original scholarly expositional text has been edited, distilled, and had its language updated and reorganized to facilitate a program of meditation and prayer. In doing so we have taken liberties with form (for example we use sense lines) and phrasing, but at all times our goal has been to remain true to her meaning.

© 2004 by Quest Associates

www.avemariapress.com

International Standard Book Number: 1-59471-026-0

Cover by Katherine Robinson Coleman

Printed and bound in the United States of America.

Library of Congress Cataloging-in-Publication Data

Kirvan, John J.
  Grace through simplicity : the practical spirituality of Evelyn Underhill / John Kirvan.
     p. cm. -- (Thirty days with a great spiritual teacher)
  ISBN 1-59471-026-0 (pbk.)
  1. Meditations. I. Underhill, Evelyn, 1875-1941. II. Title. III. Series: 30 days with a great spiritual teacher.

  BV4832.3.K57 2004
  242'.2--dc22

                              2004006265

Evelyn Underhill
(1875–1941)

When Evelyn Underhill wrote in the late 1930s that her "object was to present some of the great truths concerning man's spiritual life in simple language" she was referring to a series of BBC radio talks, but she could have been summarizing her life's work and indeed the changing face of western spirituality. Spirituality was for her, as it has become for most seekers, not "an intense form of other-worldliness remote from the common ways and incompatible with the common life, but rather the heart of religion and therefore of vital concern to ordinary men and women."

It is a vision worth prayerful attention.

For openers: it was a woman—and not a woman religious—who wrote these lines. First raised by, and then married to, London barristers, her life was anything but cloistered. In theory and in action she rejected other-worldliness as the matter and destination of the spiritual journey. She never separated world and spirit. "We are created," she wrote "in another place, both in time and in eternity, not truly one, but truly two; and every thought, word, and act must be subdued to the dignity of that double situation."

She talks of common ways and common life. There is for her no flight into another world or even into spiritually privileged safe-havens where our faltering humanity can be protected from itself.

For her, spirituality must be compatible with ordinary life—the kind of life that most of us live. It is not an accident that the heart of her spiritual insight—and this book—is a journey into Reality rather than the escape that marks so much spiritual teaching and writing.

Nor was it an accident that she spelled out her credo in a radio studio to be heard in the family parlor, in a nation on the edge of war.

8

All this is far more radical than it may appear in the early years of another century where our too easy response is often: "Of course. Been there for a long time now. Done that. What's next?"

Most important perhaps, in understanding her life and work, is a word that may not appear above but which was the focal point of her writings and speaking. The word is *mysticism*—"one of the most abused words in the English language." The abuse continues. But in that one word, too often reserved for the spiritually privileged when it is not being debased as a synonym for magic, she professed and taught her belief that holiness is not for the few, but is rather an invitation extended to all. It involves not a retreat into a silent soul, but a reaching out to a noisy world, a reaching out that is best done hand in hand with your fellow "mystics."

In 1911 she published *Mysticism,* an extraordinary work that established her reputation for clear thinking and writing. It remains in print. Four years later she published *Practical Mysticism*, adding an adjective that firmly rooted her kind of spirituality in our everyday world.

In this book she defined mysticism as "the art of union with Reality," and the mystic as "a person who has attained that union in greater or lesser degree; or who aims at and believes in such attainment." It is a definition that includes great saints and stumbling seekers. Without ever dumbing down the richness of the western mystical tradition, she has made it accessible to seekers of every tradition and personal history. She has helped us to understand our mysterious journey, even as she provides encouragement and nourishment along the way.

What makes her writings resonate today is her conviction that mysticism and the spiritual life as a whole are not separatist, not a rejection of our humanity but a journey into its fullness, into Reality. Dana Greene puts it this way: in the writings and life of Evelyn Underhill "each person is called to participate in the spiritual life, to be filled up with the object of love itself, God."

This is the art of union with Reality and with our fellow seekers. Spirituality remains "the heart of religion and therefore of vital concern to ordinary men and women."

How to Pray This Book

The purpose of this book is to open a gate, to make accessible the spiritual experience and wisdom of one of the modern world's most important spiritual scholars and teachers, Evelyn Underhill.

This is, therefore, not a book for mere reading. It invites you to meditate and pray its words on a daily basis over a period of thirty days.

It is a handbook for a spiritual journey.

Before you read these spiritual "guidelines," remember that this book is meant to free your spirit, not confine it. If on any day the meditation does not resonate well for you, turn elsewhere to find a passage that seems to best fit the spirit of your day and your soul. Don't hesitate to repeat a day as often as you like until you feel that you have discovered what the Spirit, through the words of the author, has to say to your spirit.

Here are suggestions on one way to use this book as a cornerstone of your prayers.

As Your Day Begins

As the day begins set aside a quiet moment in a quiet place to read the meditation suggested for the day.

The passage is short. It never runs more than a couple of hundred words, but it has been carefully selected to give a spiritual focus, a spiritual center to your whole day. It is designed to remind you as another day begins of your own existence at a spiritual level. It is meant to put you in the presence of the spiritual master who is your companion and teacher on this journey. But most of all the purpose of the passage is to remind you that at this moment and at every moment during this day you will be living and acting in the presence of a God who invites you continually, but quietly, to live in and through him.

A word of advice: read slowly. Very slowly. The meditation has been broken down into sense lines to help you do just this. Don't read to get to the end, but to savor each part of the meditation. You never know what short phrase, what word will trigger a response in your spirit. Give the words a chance. After all, you are not just reading this passage, you are praying it. You are establishing a mood of serenity for your whole day. What's the rush?

All Through Your Day

Immediately following the day's reading, you will find a single sentence, which we have chosen to call a mantra, a word borrowed from the Hindu tradition, but now in wide use in the

West. This phrase is meant as a companion for your spirit as it moves through a busy day. Write it down on a 3" x 5" card or on the appropriate page of your daybook. Look at it as often as you can. Repeat it quietly to yourself—and go on your way.

It is not meant to stop you in your tracks or to distract you from responsibilities, but simply, gently, to remind you of the presence of God and your desire to respond to this presence.

As Your Day Is Ending

This is a time for letting go of the day.

Find a quiet place and calm your spirit. Breath deeply. Inhale, exhale—slowly and deliberately, again and again until you feel your body let go of its tension.

Now read the evening prayer slowly, phrase by phrase. You will recognize at once that we have woven into it phrases taken from the meditation with which you began your day and the mantra that has accompanied you all through your day. In this way, a simple evening prayer gathers together the spiritual character of the day that is now ending as it began—in the presence of God.

It is a time for summary and closure.

Invite God to embrace you with love and to protect you through the night.

Sleep well.

Some Other Ways to Use This Book

1. Use it any way your spirit suggests. As mentioned earlier, skip a passage that doesn't resonate for you on a given day, or repeat for a second day or even several days a passage whose richness speaks to you. The truths of a spiritual life are not absorbed in a day, or for that matter, in a lifetime. So take your time. Be patient with the Lord. Be patient with yourself.

2. Take two passages and/or their mantras—the more contrasting the better—and "bang" them together. Spend time discovering how their similarities or differences illumine your path.

3. Start a spiritual journal to record and deepen your experience of this thirty-day journey. Using either the mantra or another phrase from the reading that appeals to you, write a spiritual account of your day, a spiritual reflection. Create your own meditation.

4. Join millions who are seeking to deepen their spiritual life by joining with others to form a small group. More and more people are doing just this to support each other in their mutual quest. Meet once a week, or at least every other week to discuss and pray about one of the meditations. There are many books and guides available to help you make such a group effective.

Thirty Days With
Evelyn Underhill

Day One

My Day Begins

Now and then
some great emotion,
some devastating visitation of beauty, love, or pain
lifts us to another level of consciousness;
and we are aware for a moment
of the difference between what seems reality to us
and the height, the depth, and the breadth
of that which is truly Real.

Our focus is sharpened,
our landscape widens to one that is
more brilliant, more significant, more detailed,
more Real.

The material for a more intense life,
a wider, sharper, consciousness,
a more profound understanding of our own existence
lies at our gates.

A more intense life awaits us.
We are invited to vitalize our latent faculties,
to arouse our languid consciousness,
to emancipate our spirit
from the fetters of appearances,
to turn our attention
to new levels of the world.

Reality exists for us all;
and we may all participate in it,
and unite with it
according to the measure,
the strength,
and the purity of our desire.

But we have to want the Reality
that invites us, that awaits us,
that except for these heightened moments
we hardly know is here.

All Through the Day

We have to want the
Reality that invites us.

My Day Is Ending

Lord,
you have been with me all through this day,
stay with me now.
As the shadows lengthen into darkness
let the noisy world grow quiet,
let its feverish concerns be stilled,
its voices silenced.
In the final moments of this day
remind me of what is Real.

If just for these quiet moments
let me be aware of the difference
between what I mistake for Reality
and the height, the depth,
and the breadth of that which is truly Real.

Sharpen my focus,
widen my landscape
to what is Real.

Let me be aware of you.

Keep me in the embrace of your Reality
through this night,
and the day to come.
Surround me with your silence
and give me the rest that only you can give—
Real peace,
now and forever.

Day Two

My Day Begins

We are created and live
both in time and in eternity,

So when St. Teresa said
that her prayer had become solid like a house,
she meant that
even though its walls rose up toward heaven
its foundations went deep down
into the lowly but firm ground of human nature,
into the concrete actualities of the natural life.

We know that our house has a ground floor,
a natural life biologically conditioned,
with animal instincts and affinities;
and that this life is very important,
for it is the product of the divine creativity
—its builder and maker is God.
But we know too
that we have an upper floor,
a supernatural life,
with supernatural possibilities,
a capacity for God;
and that this,
humankind's peculiar prerogative,
is more important still.

If we try to live on one level alone
we destroy
the mysterious beauty of our human vocation;
so utterly a part
of the fugitive and creaturely life of this planet
and yet so deeply colored by eternity;
entirely one with the world of nature,
and yet "in the spirit,"
a habitation of God.

All Through the Day

We are entirely one with the world,
yet a habitation for God.

My Day Is Ending

Lord,
you have been with me all through this day,
stay with me now.
As the shadows lengthen into darkness
let the noisy world grow quiet,
let its feverish concerns be stilled,
its voices silenced.
In the final moments of this day
remind me of what is Real.

But let me not forget
that you were as present in
the stresses of the day just past

as you are now
in the silence of this night.

You have made me for
day and for night,
for work and for rest,
for both heaven and earth.

Here in this night
let me embrace and not regret
the mysterious beauty of my humanity.
Keep me in the embrace of your Reality through the night,
and the day to come.
Surround me with your silence
and give me the rest that only you can give—
Real peace,
now and forever.

Day Three

My Day Begins

The Real mystical life,
which is the truly practical life,
begins at the beginning;
not with supernatural acts and ecstatic apprehensions,
but with the normal faculties of the average person.
As we take our first steps
on the pathway to Reality
we are not required
as Teresa told her meditation pupils,

to form great and esoteric considerations
in our understanding.

"I require of you," she said,
"no more than to look"
—to look not for something new,
not to peer into the depths of things,
but only to gaze
with a new and cleansed vision
on the ordinary,
to reexamine the furniture of our lives
to take a more starry view of them.

It is time to stand back
from the whirl of the earth
and observe the process of things.

However concrete they may appear,
there lies a universal truth
behind their every detail.

Within the most rational propositions
the meditative eye
may glimpse a dream.

It is there for the looking.

All Through the Day

Reality is there for the looking.

My Day Is Ending

Lord,
you have been with me all through this day,
stay with me now.
As the shadows lengthen into darkness
let the noisy world grow quiet,
let its feverish concerns be stilled,
its voices silenced.
In the final moments of this day
remind me of what is Real.

It is time for me to stand back
from the whirl of the earth
and observe the process of things.

However concrete they may appear,
there lies a universal truth
behind their every detail.

Within the most rational propositions
the meditative eye
may glimpse a dream.

Keep me in the embrace of your Reality through this night,
and the day to come.
Surround me with your silence
and give me the rest that only you can give—
Real peace,
now and forever.

Day Four

My Day Begins

It is in prayer and meditation
that we will discover
in our inmost sanctuary
a self, an "I,"
not wholly practical,
who refuses to be satisfied by our busy life,
a self who hungers for communion
with a spiritual universe.

And this being
so foreign to our surface consciousness,
yet familiar to it
and continuous with it,
we will recognize as our true self
whose existence
we have taken for granted
but whom we have only hitherto known
only in scattered manifestations;
it is the Real "I."

We will find our self, our "I,"
by penetrating
the constantly changing appearance of things,
our busy unstable consciousness
with its moods and obsessions,

its feverish alternations of interest and apathy,
its conflicts and irrational impulses,
which even the psychologists
mistake for "I."
We will at last discover
our own deeper being,
our eternal spark,
the agent of all our contacts with Reality,

We have read about it,
now we will meet it;
now we will know for a fact
that Reality is there.

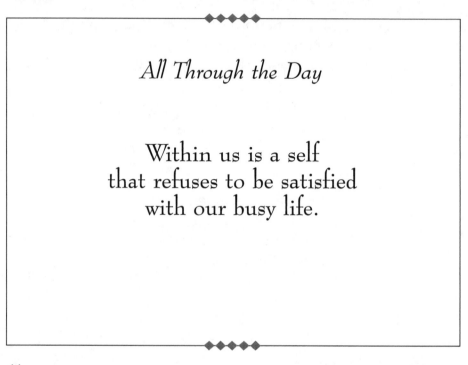

All Through the Day

Within us is a self
that refuses to be satisfied
with our busy life.

My Day Is Ending

Lord,
you have been with me all through this day,
stay with me now.
As the shadows lengthen into darkness
let the noisy world grow quiet,
let its feverish concerns be stilled,
its voices silenced.
In the final moments of this day
remind me of what is Real.

Bring me face to face
With my true self.

In the silence of this night
let me hear and heed
that part of me
that can never be satisfied
with the business of my day,
that deeper self,
that eternal spark
that hungers for Reality.

Keep me in the embrace of that Reality
through this night,
and the day to come.
Surround me with your silence
and give me the rest that only you can give—
Real peace,
now and forever.

Day Five

My Day Begins

Reality is with us,
inviting our contemplation perpetually,
but we are, to be honest,
more often than not
too frightened,
lazy, and suspicious
to respond.
We are too arrogant to still our thought,
and let Reality in,
to let God have his way.

Our vision is hung
with the cobwebs of thought:
prejudice, cowardice, sloth.

Our soul needs
a veritable spring cleaning,
a turning out,
a rearrangement
of our mental furniture,
a wide opening of closed windows,
so that the notes of the wild birds
beyond our garden
may come to us
fully charged with wonder and freshness,
and drown with their music
the noise of the gramophone within.

To open our soul to Reality
requires industry and good will.
But work at it and we will discover
that we have been living
in a stuffy world
whilst our inheritance
was a world of morning glory
where every tit-mouse
is a celestial messenger,
and every thrusting bud
is charged with the full significance of life.

All Through the Day

Reality is with us
but we are too frightened to respond.

My Day Is Ending

Lord,
you have been with me all through this day,
stay with me now.
As the shadows lengthen into darkness
let the noisy world grow quiet,
let its feverish concerns be stilled,
its voices silenced.
In the final moments of this day
remind me of what is Real.

I am, I admit,
too frightened, too lazy, and too suspicious
to respond to your invitation
to a richer life,
too arrogant

to let Reality in,
to let you have your way.

But here in this silent night,
if just for the moments left in this day
help me let go of the musty world
I seem to prefer,
and at least for these moments
claim my inheritance of life.

Keep me in the embrace of your Reality
through this night,
and the day to come.
Surround me with your silence
and give me the rest that only you can give—
Real peace,
now and forever.

Day Six

My Day Begins

The more we meditate
the more, that is, we look,
the more the busy hum of the world
becomes a distant exterior melody,
and the more we realize
that in some way
we are already withdrawing from that busy world.

Between it and us.
we are setting a ring of silence.

And in that silence we are becoming free.

We now look at a multi-colored world
and it seems to be
only a thin and papery image
of a deeper life
that is still beyond our reach.

Gradually we become aware of an entity,
an *"I"*
who can now hold at arm's length,
be aware of,
look at,
an idea
—a universe—
other than itself.

In this act of looking,
in this moment of recollection,
we are saying "no"
to the world's total claim to our consciousness.

We are taking a first step on a ladder that
—as the mystics say—
goes from multiplicity to unity.

In some way
we are withdrawing
from the grip of unrealities,
from notions and concepts
with which until now
we have been content.

Now the values of our existence are changed.
"The road to a Yea lies through a Nay."

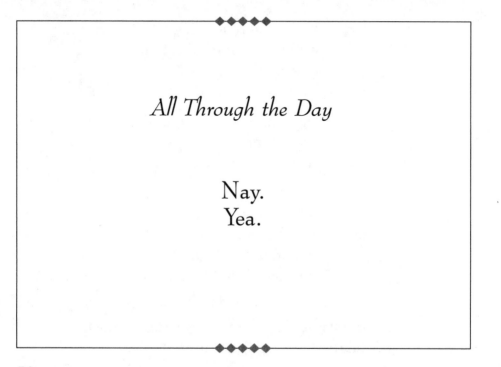

All Through the Day

Nay.
Yea.

My Day Is Ending

Lord,
you have been with me all through this day,
stay with me now.
As the shadows lengthen into darkness
let the noisy world grow quiet,
let its feverish concerns be stilled,
its voices silenced.
In the final moments of this day
remind me of what is Real,
what lies beneath
the multicolored surface of my world.

Build around me
in the closing moments of this day

a ring of silence
that will free me from the grip
of unrealities,
from notions and concepts
with which until now
I have been content.

Keep me rather
in the embrace of your Reality
through this night,
and the day to come.
Surround me with your silence
and give me the rest that only you can give—
Real peace,
now and forever.

Day Seven

―

My Day Begins

We need to take a fresh look at our self,
to see our self in a fresh relationship with things.
We need to surrender our self willingly
to the moods of astonishment, humility, joy
—perhaps of deep shame or sudden love—
which will invade our heart even as we look.

If we do this patiently, day after day,
constantly recapturing our wandering attention,
ever renewing the struggle for simplicity of sight,

we will at last discover
that there us something within us,
something that is behind, and beyond
the fractious, conflicting life of desire.
There is something that we can recall
and gather up.
Something out of which we can
make a new life.
We will in fact
know our own soul for the first time.
We will learn
that in some sense this Real "I"
is distinct from and alien to
the world in which we find our self.

We are like actors
who have another life when we are not onstage.

When we do not merely believe this
but know it,
when we have acquired this power
of withdrawing our self,
of making the first distinction
between appearance and Reality,

the initial stage of our contemplative life has begun.

The Real world awaits us.

All Through the Day

The struggle is to see clearly.

My Day Is Ending

Lord,
you have been with me all through this day,
stay with me now.
As the shadows lengthen into darkness
let the noisy world grow quiet,
let its feverish concerns be stilled,
its voices silenced.
In the final moments of this day
remind me of what is Real.

Remind me
with every passing day that
appearance is not Reality,
that there is something within me
and all around me

that goes beyond
all the struggles and conflicting desires of this day,
something that I can recall
day after day,
something out of which I can
make a new life
and come to know
my own soul for the first time.
Keep me in the embrace of your Reality
throughout this night,
and the day to come.
Surround me with your silence
and give me the rest that only you can give—
Real peace,
now and forever.

Day Eight

My Day Begins

The climb up the mountain of self-knowledge
is a lonely and arduous excursion
that will test our courage and sincerity.

Most of us will prefer
to dwell in comfortable ignorance
on its lower slopes
content to live with the hard truths
heavily veiled.

Few of us can bear
to contemplate ourselves face to face,
because what we see
could be strange and terrifying.

To look at ourselves
means stripping our motives bare
and measuring them against eternal values.

It means looking squarely at
our unacknowledged self-indulgences,
our irrational loves and hates.

It compels us
to remodel our whole existence
and become for the first time
a practical person,
someone in touch with Reality.

It is a vision
that will forever change us.
It forces us
to adopt a new attitude toward ourselves
and all other things.

Our climb up the mountain of self-knowledge
is conversion
at the deepest level of our being.

But only at the summit of this mountain
do we discover
the beginning of the
the pathway to Reality.

All Through the Day

Getting to know ourselves
is always a lonely and arduous journey.

My Day Is Ending

Lord,
you have been with me all through this day,
stay with me now.
As the shadows lengthen into darkness
let the noisy world grow quiet,
let its feverish concerns be stilled,
its voices silenced.

I need you to remind me again
that though I would prefer
to dwell in comfortable ignorance
and live with the hard truths
of my journey heavily veiled,
there is no easy road

up the mountain of self-knowledge.
If I am to become for the first time
a practical person,
someone in touch with Reality,
there is no escape from
remodeling my whole existence.

I need you to keep me
in the embrace of your Reality through this night,
and all the days to come.
Give me the courage that only you can give—
Real courage,
now and forever.

Day Nine

My Day Begins

Here on the mountain
we discover how deeply tied we have been
to an unreal world.

Our energy has been turned
in the wrong direction for too long,
harnessed to the wrong machine.
We have become accustomed to wanting,
to thinking that we need the right portfolio,
the right car, the right address, the right spouse,
all the right trophies.

Old habits have us in chains.
We have not been free.

But here on the mountain
we are suddenly awake to the struggle
between the simple, insistent longings of our surface self,
and the equally simple longings and instincts
of our long buried spirit
which is now beginning
to assert itself,
pushing out, as it were,
toward the light.

We are discovering at last
our own deeper being,
our eternal spark,
our deeper self.

In this moment
our old habits may appear childish,
unworthy and absurd.
But we can't stop at simple recognition.

The moment demands of us
nothing less
than a drastic remodeling of our character.

All Through the Day

Freedom beckons.

My Day Is Ending

Lord,
you have been with me all through this day,
stay with me now.
As the shadows lengthen into darkness
let the noisy world grow quiet,
let its feverish concerns be stilled,
its voices silenced.
In the final moments of this day
remind me of what is Real.

Breaking the chains
that bind me to an unreal world
will not be easy.
I am too comfortable here.

But there is within me
a long buried spirit
which is now beginning
to assert itself,
pushing out, as it were,
toward the light.
Help me to get out of its way.

Keep me in the embrace of your Reality
through this night,
and the day to come.
Surround me with your silence
and give me the rest that only you can give—
Real peace,
now and forever.

Day Ten

My Day Begins

We are neither angel nor animal.
We are capable of
directing our lives to either eternity or time.
But it is one thing
to frame beautiful theories on these subjects.
It is another to live out the tension
in our own lives.

We know the discomfort of
being pulled two ways at once.
Our attention vacillates
between two incompatible ideals.

We can be convinced on the one hand
that there is something wrong,
perverse, and poisonous about life
as we have always lived it.
On the other hand we can be just as convinced
that there is something hopelessly ethereal
about the life
that our innermost inhabitant wants to live.
First one and then the other asserts itself.

We fluctuate miserably
between their attractions and their claims.
We will have no peace until these claims are met
and the apparent opposition between them resolved.

But here on the mountain
we have become certain

that there is another, more durable
and more "reasonable" life possible
than the one on which we have spent our energies.

We have begun to know
and feel in every fiber of our being
the mystical need for union with Reality,
and to realize that the values
that we have accepted so trustfully
cannot keep their promises
to give us what we most desire.

But it also has become clear to us
that if we are to achieve this other life,
if we are to dwell in it and breathe its air,
we must become more than we are now.

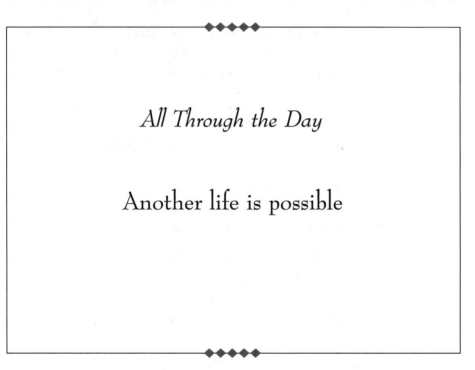

All Through the Day

Another life is possible

My Day Is Ending

Lord,
you have been with me all through this day,
stay with me now.
As the shadows lengthen into darkness
let the noisy world grow quiet,
let its feverish concerns be stilled,
its voices silenced.
In the final moments of this day
remind me of what is Real.

There are moments during the day
when I feel close to the angels,
and others when I am closer
to the animal in my soul.
But I am neither; I am both.

I live in time and in eternity.
I am pulled two ways.
I could go either.
But one thing is certain: a better life beckons.
And this is certain: if I want to live there,
if I want to breathe its air,
I will have to become more than I am now.

So keep me in the embrace of your Reality through this night,
and all the days to come.
Let me choose the life that only you can give—
Real peace,
now and forever.

Day Eleven

My Day Begins

We can become like limpets
clinging persistently
to what we have and where we are.
exchanging freedom
for apparent security,
a rich stream of life
for a defensive shell of fixed ideas.

Our mind is full of little whirlpools,
twists and currents, conflicting systems,
incompatible desires.

One after another
we center our lives on
ambition, love, duty, friendship,
social conventions, politics, religion—
one self-interest after another.

And one after another
these things either fail us or enslave us.

They can become obsessions
distorting our judgement, narrowing our outlook,
coloring our whole existence,
Involving us in public difficulties, private compromises,
and self-deception of every kind.

This state of affairs
which usually passes for "an active life,"

looks very different
when viewed with the simple meditative eye.
We see it as the muddle it is
and we realize that we are neither strong enough
or clever enough to undo it.

Like the limpet we have become
we will have to be detached from our comfort,
not by kind words, but by main force.
Our old clinging life, protected by our hard shell
from the living waters of the sea, must come to an end.
Old habits, old notions, old prejudices
will have to be severed.

All Through the Day

Too often we exchange freedom
for apparent security.

My Day Is Ending

Lord,
you have been with me all through this day,
stay with me now.
As the shadows lengthen into darkness
let the noisy world grow quiet,
let its feverish concerns be stilled,
its voices silenced.

I have exchanged freedom
for apparent security,
a rich stream of life
for a defensive shell of fixed ideas.

Like the limpet I have become,
I will have to be detached from my comfort,

not by kind words but by main force.
My old clinging life
must come to an end.
Old habits, old notions, old prejudices
will have to be severed.
But I realize that I am neither strong enough
nor clever enough to pull free.

So keep me in the embrace of your Reality
through this night,
and all the days to come.
Let me choose the freedom that only you can give—
Real freedom,
now and forever.

GRACE THROUGH SIMPLICITY

Day Twelve

My Day Begins

Ascending the mountain of self-knowledge
requires two things:
jettisoning the unreal
and focusing all our energies
on the Real.

Only by leaving behind our superfluous baggage
will we arrive at the point
that the mystics call the summit of the spirit,
where the various forces of our character
—our energy, our intellect, our desirous heart—

so easily and so long dissipated
amongst a thousand little wants and preferences
are gathered into one
to become a strong and disciplined instrument
wherewith our true self
can force a path deeper and deeper
into the heart of Reality.

It is only by setting aside
our feverish attachment to things
—our need to possess—
that we will ever achieve that mental attitude
that the mystics sometimes call poverty
and sometimes perfect freedom.

It is a question of
unifying and simplifying our lives,

choosing from among
the conflicting passions, interests and desires
of our heart and soul,
in order to devote all our energies
to establishing one center to our lives.

If we are to succeed in this adventure
there must be no frittering of energy,
no mixture of motives,
but rather
a purgation of our heart.

All Through the Day

With one heart. . . .

My Day Is Ending

Lord,
you have been with me all through this day,
stay with me now.
As the shadows lengthen into darkness
let the noisy world grow quiet,
let its feverish concerns be stilled,
its voices silenced.

In the silence of this night
gather up the thousand things
that have caught my attention
and distracted my heart,
and make of them one prayer, one soul.

Take the baggage
that weighs down my soul and my life,
that clutters even this quiet moment.
Let me leave it behind,
as I enter the dark silence of this night,
Let me enter your presence
with a simpler heart
and undistracted soul.

So keep me in the embrace of your Reality
through this night,
and all the days to come.

Day Thirteen

My Day Begins

If we experience a fundamental opposition
between the things of this world
and those of the spirit
it is a conflict we have created for ourselves.

The problem is not in the things themselves,
but in our self-created attitude toward them…
an attitude to "things" that
consists of demands, appetites, wants,
an enslavement to the verb "to have,"
with its quiet certitude

that we are well within our rights
in pushing the claims of "the *I*, the *Me*, the *Mine*."

We are driven by a demand
either for a continued possession of what we have,
or for something
which as yet we do not have:
wealth, honor, success, social position, love, friendship,
comfort, amusement.

We are convinced that we have a right
to have our abilities recognized
to be immune from failure or humiliation.
We come to resent anything that stands in our way.
We are upset when others prove themselves
more skillful than we are in the game of acquisition.

These attitudes,
so ordinary that they can pass unnoticed,
have a name given to them by our blunt forefathers—
they are the Seven Deadly Sins of
Pride, Anger, Envy, Avarice, Sloth, Gluttony and Lust.

As long as these egotistical attitudes
govern our character,
we can never see or feel things as they are,
but only as they affect ourselves.

This is why the mystics tell us perpetually
that "self-centeredness must be killed
before Reality be attained."

All Through the Day

It is not "things," it is us.

My Day Is Ending

Lord,
you have been with me all through this day,
stay with me now.
As the shadows lengthen into darkness
let the noisy world grow quiet,
let its feverish concerns be stilled.
In the silence of this night
let me recognize
how deep is my need for "things,"
how driven is my soul
to protect what I have,
how hungry I am for what I "want,"
for what I think I need.

I know that as long as I
blind myself to anything
beyond my own needs
I will never see or feel things as they are.
I will live with the unreal,
Reality beyond my reach,
locked into the "deadening" sins
of my own need "to have."

Here in the silent darkness of this night
break through my blindness,
cut away at what is not Real,
the ridiculous megalomania
that makes me the center of my universe.

Embrace me with your Reality.

Day Fourteen

My Day Begins

Only the Real, say the mystics,
can know Reality.

We behold that which we are.
The universe we see
is conditioned by the character of the mind
that sees it.
And since what we seek
is no mere glimpse of eternal life,
no mere glimpse of Reality,

but complete possession of it,
every part of us—
the rich totality of our character,
all the forces of our soul
not just some thin and isolated
spiritual side of our character—
must be Real.

But to be Real,
to be assured of Reality,
we need to retreat constantly
to the quiet center of our spirit.
Only in this recollection, this focusing,
will we find the support we need
to carry us through the pain and stress

of the self-simplification
that our pursuit of Reality demands.

Only this silent recollection,
joined to our perpetual efforts
at self-adjustment,
can permit us to hope on
in the teeth of the world's inevitable
cruelty and indifference.

To the extent that we become Real,
only to that same extent
do we know Reality.

All Through the Day

Only the Real can know Reality.

My Day Is Ending

Lord,
you have been with me all through this day,
stay with me now.
As the shadows lengthen into darkness
let the noisy world grow quiet,
let its feverish concerns be stilled.
In the silence of this night
let me recognize
that until I become Real
your Reality will escape me.

What I seek
is no mere glimpse of eternal life,
no mere glimpse of your Reality,

but to be possessed by it,
by you.

Make Real,
by your presence,
every part of my life.

Keep me in your embrace
through this night,
and in all the days to come,
be my Reality.

Day Fifteen

My Day Begins

It is important not to confuse our pursuit of Reality
with dreaminess and idle musing.
This pursuit is not abject surrender of reason
to every passing "mystical" impression.
It is not sentimental aestheticism
or emotional piety.

It is rather
an intense effort to extend our vision,
a passionate and self-forgetful act of communion.

It is, says one old English mystic,
"a blind intent stretching——a privy love pressed."
It is to move in the direction of Ultimate Beauty,
thwarting all the checks, hindrances, and contradictions
of the restless world.
It is a "loving stretching out" toward Reality,
a pressing outward of our whole personality,
an eager and trustful stretching
toward the fresh universe that awaits us.

It requires of us that we transcend reason,
that we push with all our power—
not to absorb new and more accurate ideas,
but rather to pour forth will and love.

"By love may he be gotten and holden.
But by thought never."

Our pursuit of Reality
is an act of love.

It is an eager outpouring of ourselves,
a wooing, not a critical study.
It is a seeking, a touching, and tasting
of the beautiful wherever it is found—
not a consideration of it, not an analysis.

It is also not something that
can ever be achieved by spiritual silliness.
To transcend reason
is not unreasonable.

All Through the Day

Reality surrenders to love not ideas.

My Day Is Ending

Lord,
you have been with me all through this day,
stay with me now.
As the shadows lengthen into darkness
let the noisy world grow quiet,
let its feverish concerns be stilled,
its voices silenced.

But don't let me, under cover of darkness,
reduce your presence
to a comforting dream,
to an idle bed-time musing
that will be gone with the dawn.
I know that you are not to be found

in every passing "mystical" impression,
in warm baths of sentiment,
but only in stretching my soul
toward the beauty of your Reality.

So I pray that you will
keep me in your embrace
through this night, and the day to come.
And that you will give me the rest
that only you can give—
Real peace,
now and forever.

Day Sixteen

My Day Begins

The heart's desire
is a better promise of possible fulfillment
than the most elegant theories of the spiritual world.

By our heart's eager out-stretching toward Reality
we tend not only to move toward Reality
but to enter into its rhythm,
and by a humble and unquestioning surrender to it
we permit its entrance into our souls.

We apprehend the Real and the eternal
as we apprehend the sunshine
when the sky is free of cloud.

If we "smite therefore
upon that thick cloud of unknowing
with a sharp dart of longing love"
—with the desire of our heart—
the cloud shall part and disclose the blue.

We will move to a new plane
where we shall see more intensely,
hear more intensely,
touch and taste more intensely
than ever before.

We begin to look out
—steadily, deliberately—

with eyes of love toward the world,
with an attitude of complete humility
and receptiveness,
without criticism,
without clever analyses of what we see.

We see things at last as an artist does,
in themselves and for their own sake.
We surrender our "I"-hood.
Everything appears as it is.
The disfiguring results of hate, rivalry, and prejudice melt
away.
New music, new color, new light
pour into our soul
from a world we are seeing for the first time.

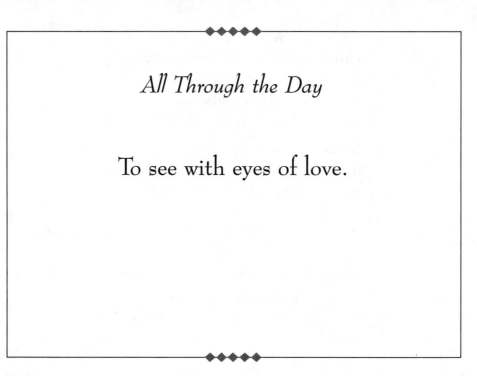

All Through the Day

To see with eyes of love.

My Day Is Ending

Lord,
you have been with me all through this day,
stay with me now.
As the shadows lengthen into darkness
let the noisy world grow quiet,
let its feverish concerns be stilled,
its voices silenced.

Let me see through
the darkness of this night
with the eyes of love.

Let me see my world
for the first time,
and let the sight of it

fill my heart this night
and for all the days to come
with its music, its color, and its light.

Keep me in your embrace
through this night, and the day to come.
Substitute your eyes for mine
and give me the sight
that only you can give—
now and forever.

Day Seventeen

My Day Begins

The love with which we look at the world,
that sees the world as it is,
will fluctuate.

For as long as we live
we are subject to change.

But the "will" that has been enkindled
by this love
will be there to keep us on track,
to keep us attuned and turned
in the direction of the best.

We can with this love-engendered will
refuse to lapse into the unreal
and the "I"-centered life
out of which it is leading us.

Toughened and trained,
detached from our unreal wants,
and merged with the love
with which we now view the world,
the "will" will be there
if we choose it,
even in darkness
and in the suffering
that such darkness brings
to our awakened spirit.

This "will" can continue to cut its way
into new levels of Reality,
becoming as it goes and grows
the primary agent
of our spiritual undertaking,
the active expression
of our deepest and purest desires,
a center out of which
we can look at the world
steadily and deliberately
with eyes of love.

All Through the Day

As long as we live
our heart is subject to change.

My Day Is Ending

Lord,
you have been with me all through this day,
stay with me now.
As the shadows lengthen into darkness
let the noisy world grow quiet,
let its feverish concerns be stilled,
its voices silenced.

Let me fix my eyes and my will
steadily and deliberately
on the new world
that I am just now beginning to see.

Bring my heart ever closer
to the Reality,
that now I only glimpse.

Even in darkness,
and in whatever suffering
that such darkness brings,
keep my spirit alive,
my eyes wide open,
my desire strong.

Keep me in your embrace
through this night,
and in all the days to come.
Be my North Star,
the Reality that strengthens my will,
that captivates my heart.

Day Eighteen

My Day Begins

Coming to see the world
in a whole new way
is gradual.

It depends not so much
on a philosophy accepted,
or a new gift of vision suddenly received,
as upon an uninterrupted changing,
a widening and deepening
of our character.

It is a progressive growth
toward the Real,
an ever more profound harmonization
of our self's life
with the greater and inclusive rhythms
of existence.

It is a perpetually renewed breaking down
of the hard barriers of individualism,
a willing submission
to the compelling rhythm
of a larger existence
than that of our individuality,
a perpetual widening, deepening,
and un-*selfing* of our attentiveness.

We seek to become citizens
of a greater, more joyous,
and more poignant world,
partakers of a more abundant life,
a life that the great mystics describe
only as a world that is "unwalled."

But this is a gradual process
that depends on breaking down those walls
that shut our "selves" off
from all the other "selves."

All Through the Day

My growth depends on the walls
coming down.

My Day Is Ending

Lord,
you have been with me all through this day,
stay with me now.
As the shadows lengthen into darkness
let the noisy world grow quiet,
let its feverish concerns be stilled,
its voices silenced.

Here in the dark silence of this night,
I know what stands between me
and the larger, more abundant, and joyous life
that my heart seeks.

The walls I have built
to protect my self

will have to come down,
so that others,
so that you
may come in.

I will have to choose
a life bigger than my self.
Keep me in your embrace,
and in the silence of this night
let the walls begin to fall.

Day Nineteen

My Day Begins

The discovery of God begins
not in some ecstatic adventure
but in a loving and patient exploration
of the world that lies at our gates.

Some of us are tempted
to elude nature,
to refuse her friendship,
attempting to leap the river of life
in the hope of finding God on the other side.

Others of us will be tempted
to deliberately arrest our development.
Attuned to the wonderful rhythms of natural life,
we are content with this increased sensibility
and become a "nature mystic " and no more.

But our hope
is in stretching out in love
toward the myriad manifestations of life
that surround us,
which in the ordinary course of things
we hardly notice
unless and until we need them.

It matters not whether it is the Alps or an insect,
provided that our attitude be right,
for all things in this world

toward which we stretch
are linked together,
and the one truly apprehended
will be the gateway to the rest.

It would be a pity
to remain ignorant of this,
to keep, as it were, a plate glass window
between us
and the world at our gate.

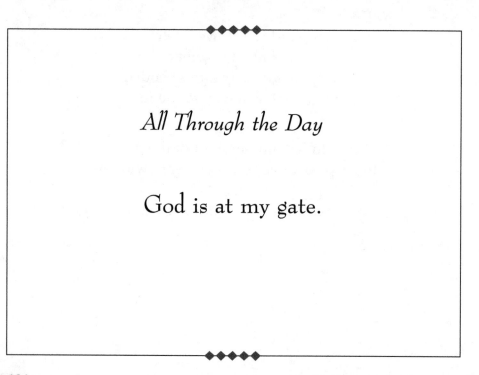

All Through the Day

God is at my gate.

My Day Is Ending

Lord,
you have been with me all through this day,
stay with me now.
As the shadows lengthen into darkness
let the noisy world grow quiet,
let its feverish concerns be stilled,
its voices silenced.

In my search for you
in the dark silence of this night
let me not ignore
what is in front of me
and all around me.

Let me neither pass by the world at my gate
nor be content with it.
Rather, let me recognize in everything
a gateway to the rest.

You are to be found in
what I usually pass by.

Keep me in your embrace,
in the dark silence
of this night,
and in the day to come
keep my eyes and my heart open to what is Real,
to what is all around me.

Day Twenty

My Day Begins

Julian of Norwich looked upon
an object as small as a hazel nut,
and saw all of creation in its fragility
and all its enduring strength.

It will last forever she said
because God loves every fragment of life.
Every finite expression of Reality
is joined to its Origin.

But to see creation as Julian saw it
is a reward,
not for self-tormenting introspection
or self-conscious aspiration,
but rather for determination,
a steady acquiescence,
a simple and loyal surrender
to the great currents of life,
a surrender that is not limp but deliberate,
a truthful self-donation, a living faith,
a pleasing stirring of love.

Neither passivity nor anxiety
will get us anywhere.
The way may be long,
but ultimate success is assured to

those who love Reality and surrender to it.

A strong tide of Transcendent Life
will inevitably invade, clarify, and uplift
the consciousness
that is open to receive it.

"Your opening and his entry," says Eckhart,
"are but one moment."

When, therefore, we put aside our preconceptions,
our self-centered scale of values,
and let intuition have its way with us,
only when we escape the single vision of the selfish,
will we begin to grasp
all that our senses were meant to be.
Only then will we see
all of creation in a hazelnut.

All Through the Day

Neither passivity nor anxiety
will get us anywhere.

My Day Is Ending

Lord,
you have been with me all through this day,
stay with me now.
As the shadows lengthen into darkness
let the noisy world grow quiet,
let its feverish concerns be stilled,
its voices silenced.

Here in the night
let me think of Julian who
could look at a hazelnut
and see the world.
I look at the world
and see only the hazelnuts,
and my self.

To see you in the world
I need to see with your eyes,
feel with your heart,

walk in your shoes.

I am far from this.
Keep me in your embrace,
in the dark silence of this night,
and in the day to come,
keep my eyes and my heart
open to what is Real.

Day Twenty-One

My Day Begins

Breaking down the fences of our personality,
merging with a larger consciousness,
we begin to learn our world
and live in it as a citizen,
as a member of a great society,
not as a mere spectator.

But the deeper we enter into
and immerse ourselves in life,
the more we expand our consciousness,
the more insistently will rumors and intimations

of a higher plane of experience,
a closer unity,
and a more complete synthesis
besiege us.

"There begins," in the words of John Ruysbroeck,
"a hunger and a thirst,
that shall never more be stilled."

Until now we have experienced the world
as a series of disconnected words and notes.
Out of them we have, as best we could,
constructed a certain coherence.

But now we reach out,
unsatisfied with anything

but the ultimate sentence,
the perfect melody.

Our craving for Something More
becomes more acute.

We want to press through and beyond
our ceaseless activities
to a fuller and more perfect union
with the substance of all that is,
knowing that this is a hunger and thirst
that shall never be stilled.

All Through the Day

Here begins a hunger and a thirst
that shall never more be stilled.

My Day Is Ending

Lord,
you have been with me all through this day,
stay with me now.
As the shadows lengthen into darkness
let the noisy world grow quiet,
let its feverish concerns be stilled,
its voices silenced.

But do not still the desire of my heart.
Rather, let me fall asleep
hungering and thirsting,
craving for Something More.

Let my heart remain
unsatisfied with anything

but the ultimate sentence,
the perfect melody.

Keep me in your embrace,
in the dark silence
of this night,
and in the day to come
keep my eyes and my heart open to what is Real.

Day Twenty-Two

My Day Begins

Only our apathy
and the feebleness of our desire
put limits on our journey
into Reality.

What we seek
does not vary,
but our receptivity does.

There is a strict relationship
between supply and demand.

The success of our
journey into Reality
will be in direct proportion
to our desire,
courage, and generosity.

Only to the extent to which
we give our self into its embrace
will we embrace Reality.

If we set limits to our self-donation
we will feel as we attain it,
not a sense of satisfaction,
but a sense of constriction.

We will not enjoy peace
until we do away with

all the banks and hedges
of our neat garden,
and exchange them
for the wilderness that is unwalled.

Until we enter into
the wild strange place of silence
where "lovers lose themselves"
Reality will evade us.

All Through the Day

We will not enjoy peace
until we enter into
the wild strange place of silence.

My Day Is Ending

Lord,
you have been with me all through this day,
stay with me now.
As the shadows lengthen into darkness
let the noisy world grow quiet,
let its feverish concerns be stilled,
its voices silenced.

In the dark silence of this night
take my hand and lead me
into the wild strange place of silence
where "lovers lose themselves."

My protected heart will not rest
until I surrender myself

into your embrace,
until I exchange my fears
for the unwalled wilderness
of your Reality.

Keep me then in your embrace,
in the dark silence
of this night,
and in the day to come
keep my eyes and my heart open to what is Real,
to your promises.

Day Twenty-Three

My Day Begins

Creation,
the whole, always changing, natural order,
with all its apparent collisions, cruelties, and waste,
springs none-the-less from an ardor,
an immeasurable love,
a perpetual donation,
that generates, upholds, and drives it.

"God made it," Julian said,
"God loves it,
and God sustains it."

Everything,
whether gracious, terrible, or malignant
is enwrapped in love,
not by mechanical necessity,
but by God's passionate desire.
Therefore nothing can be really mean,
nothing despicable,
nothing however perverted, irredeemable.

It is a false mysticism,
blasphemy,
to conceive of the world as evil,
something to be fled from.

On the contrary
the more beautiful and noble
things appear to us,

the more we love them,
the more truly do we see them.

We see in the world,
in all things,
the love of God surging up from within.

We share with saints and poets
that simplicity and purity of vision
that allows us to see all things
"as they are in God."

All Through the Day

God made the world,
God loves it,
God sustains it.

My Day Is Ending

Lord,
you have been with me all through this day,
stay with me now.
As the shadows lengthen into darkness
let the noisy world grow quiet,
let its feverish concerns be stilled,
its voices silenced.

You made me,
you love me,
you sustain me.

What else do I need to remember?

Keep me in your embrace,
in the dark silence
of this night,
and in the day to come
keep my eyes and my heart open to what is Real.

Day Twenty-Four

My Day Begins

Reality,
as the mystics say,
is both near and far.

It is far from
and beyond our capacity and
need to imagine,
but it saturates and supports our lives.

"We dwell in him and he in us."

We participate in the Divine Order now.

There is something in us
that endures and transcends
the world of change.
It is an instinct
for another world of Reality,
a capacity for the infinite.

But we have been busy since childhood
with other matters.
All the urgent affairs of "life"
as we absurdly call it,
have monopolized our consciousness.

The really important events of our life,
all those delicate movements

that mark our inner growth
go unnoticed by us.

All this time
we have been kept and nourished
by an enfolding and creative love
but we have been and remain
less conscious of it
than we are of the air we breathe.

All Through the Day

I have a capacity for the infinite.

My Day Is Ending

Lord,
you have been with me all through this day,
stay with me now.
As the shadows lengthen into darkness
let the noisy world grow quiet,
let its feverish concerns be stilled,
its voices silenced.

Make room in my heart
for another world of Reality,
beyond the "real world" of this day.
Expand my heart's desire
to a what lies beyond the changeable.

Open my eyes to what is really important,
all those delicate movements
of your presence
that go unnoticed by me.

Keep me in your embrace,
in the dark silence of this night,
and in the day to come.
Keep my eyes and my heart open to what is Real.

Day Twenty-Five

My Day Begins

There comes that time
and that place
for which we have long hungered and thirsted.
It is a place and a time where and when
we will find ourselves emptied and free,
stripped bare of all the machinery of thought.

It is a time and place of simplicity,
a condition that the great mystics describe as
nakedness of spirit
and which they declare
to be a state of consciousness

above all images and ideas—
in which "all the workings of reason fail."

We have entered
into an intense and vivid silence
that exists in itself
through and in spite of
the ceaseless noises of the world
around and within us.

It is a silence within which
we can lose ourselves,
in whose ebb and flow
we are able to wander
lost in an imageless world.

But in spite of living
where reason and images are not enough,

GRACE THROUGH SIMPLICITY

We know that this is
where we want and need to be.
We begin to understand
what the psalmist meant when he said:
"Be still and know that I am God."

We may feel lost in this wilderness,
in this solitude where we are speechless.
But this wilderness,
desolate from one point of view,
is from another the home we sought.

It calls forth from us
the deepest adoration of which we are capable.
And though perhaps never has our soul been so active,
it seems to us that we are still at last.
At last we are at rest.

All Through the Day

Be still at last.

My Day Is Ending

Lord,
you have been with me all through this day,
stay with me now.
As the shadows lengthen into darkness
let the noisy world grow quiet,
let its feverish concerns be stilled,
its voices silenced.

I know that this
at long last is
where I want and need to be.
I am beginning to understand
what the psalmist meant when he said:
"Be still and know that I am God."

I am empty and free
in a place and a time of simplicity
where I am stripped bare
of my need for ideas and images.

I have found at last
the home I have so long sought.

Keep me in your embrace,
in the dark silence
of this night,
and in the day to come
keep my eyes and my heart open to what is Real.

Day Twenty-Six

My Day Begins

We must not presume
that our spiritual journey will lead us
to an untroubled life
supported by pleasant spiritual companions,
quietly occupying our self
in mild contemplation of the great world
through which we move.

It is to vigor rather than to comfort that we are called.

It is said of the shepherd
that he carries the lambs in his bosom,
but the sheep are expected to walk,
and to put up with the inequalities of the road,
the bunts and blunders of the flock.

We are still the sheep
blundering our way along the path.

But we are no longer just members of a flock,
driven along the road,
unaware of anything lying beyond the hedges,
ignorant of our destination,
our personal initiative and responsibility
limited to snatching some grass
as we go along,
pushing our way to the softer side of the track.

We may still be immersed in the group,
but we see things differently.
We have new ideas of what is Real.
A quiet and complete transformation,
a strengthening and maturing of our personality
has taken place.

No longer do we go blindly along with the flock.
The crowd has lost its grasp on us.
We have entered a new, wide world,
that is not just a way of seeing,
but a new way of living.

Living with Reality
we become more Real.

All Through the Day

We are called to vigor, not comfort

My Day Is Ending

Lord,
you have been with me all through this day,
stay with me now.
As the shadows lengthen into darkness
let the noisy world grow quiet,
let its feverish concerns be stilled,
its voices silenced.

But do not let me be fooled
by the comforting silence of this night.
You have not promised
untroubled days
and nights.

It is not to comfort
that you are calling me
but to let you
challenge my soul,
to transform, strengthen, and mature
every corner of my day and night

You have brought me to a new, wide world,
that is not just a way of seeing,
but a new way of living.

Keep me in your embrace,
in the dark silence
of this night,
and in the day to come
keep my eyes and my heart open to what is Real.

Day Twenty-Seven

My Day Begins

Because it is true about everything else in our lives,
it is all too easy for us to presume
that spiritual growth is about getting to know God better.
But it is not about knowing more or knowing differently.

It is about an utterly different way of living.

A vivid new life is springing up within us,
uniting our life to the life of God.
Some mystics call it a "transforming union"
—transforming because it changes everything.

We are a changed person living in a world
that we see differently.
We are more human,
more a person than we have ever been before.

We feel within ourselves a new creative freedom,
a fuller actualization of our self.

At the same time
we experience a different sense of the world,
a love and an energy upon which we come to depend.

We have become fully human,
capable for the first time
of living—in the midst of time,
the Real life of eternity.

Rather than abandoning creation
we are united with a larger, deeper, broader world.

Each little event,
is now seen in its true proportion,
because we bring to it
our new awareness of the Whole.

Things no longer rule us.
Our world has been transformed.

All Through the Day

Our world—my life—
has been transformed.

My Day Is Ending

Lord,
you have been with me all through this day.
Stay with me now.
as the shadows lengthen into darkness
let the noisy world grow quiet,
let its feverish concerns be stilled,
its voices silenced.

Let me wake to a new day,
to a new world,
to an utterly different way of living,
to a life united to yours.

I feel a new life is springing up within me.
It promises

that I can be more human,
that I can be more of a person
than I have ever been.

I can become more fully human,
capable for the first time
of living—in the midst of time
—the Real life of eternity.

Keep your promises, I beg you.

Keep me in your embrace,
in the dark silence
of this night,
and in the day to come
keep my eyes and my heart
open to what is Real.

Day Twenty-Eight

My Day Begins

Contemplation and action
are not opposites,
but two interdependent forms of a life
that is one.

We have not come this long way
only to turn our backs on creation,
but rather to reveal its meaning—
the mercy, order, and beauty
at its heart.

We have come to mend what we find broken,
to provide where we find need.
We are called not to abandon our everyday world
but to display and celebrate its deeper Reality.

Sometimes it will call us
to great, even heroic actions,
but mostly it will mean
nothing more dramatic
than meeting the small, everyday demands and opportunities
of our work-a-day world,
the perpetual give and take of our ordinary life.

We are called to live out a life that is at once ordinary
but more Real
and to make that Reality more visible,
to release its creative energy
within the world of ordinary time and space.

We are not called to rest
but to a life of passion,
to a life of active love and service.
That alone reflects
the inexhaustibly rich Reality
that we find only in God.

We are not meant to live the life
of a "dreamy mystic."
We are meant to be
active and impassioned servants
of Eternal Wisdom.

We are meant
to live a life of passionate communion
with the true and the beautiful,
with what is Real.

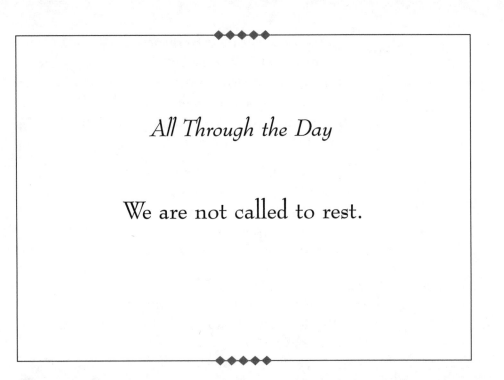

All Through the Day

We are not called to rest.

My Day Is Ending

Lord,
you have been with me all through this day,
stay with me now.
As the shadows lengthen into darkness
let the noisy world grow quiet,
let its feverish concerns be stilled,
its voices silenced.

But let me remember
that I have not been called to a life of rest,
but to a life of passion,
to a life of active love and service that reflects
the inexhaustibly rich Reality
that I can find only in you.

I am not meant to live the life
of a "dreamy mystic."
I am meant to be
your active and impassioned servant.
I am meant
to live a life of passionate communion
with the true and the beautiful, with what is Real.

With you.

Keep me in your embrace,
in the dark silence of this night,
and in the day to come
keep my eyes and my heart open to what is Real.

Day Twenty-Nine

My Day Begins

Our journey has been a long one.
It has, it seems, been all about
hardships and obstacles.

But now there is no need to push on any further.
There is no more we can do for ourselves.

We have come to a strange and bewildering place
that lies far beyond the horizon of our thought,
that lies far beyond what we can do for ourselves.

There are no familiar landmarks here,
nothing that we can cling to.
Nothing that we can achieve.

We've never been here before.
We feel lost.

"We wander to and fro," as the mystics would say
in "a fathomless ground, "
surrounded by silence and darkness.

But it is to reach this Dark Night of the Spirit
that we have journeyed so far.

We need ask for nothing,
seek nothing.

We need only keep our doors flung wide open toward God.

We will come to understand and accept
that it will be in this enveloping darkness
that we will find
that for which we have been seeking from the first—
the final Reality,
the perfect satisfaction
of our most ardent and sacred desires.

We will also come to understand and accept
that it is not our efforts
that have brought us here.
It is the most painful moment
in the growth of our soul.
But it is also the most essential.

All Through the Day

I am a stranger in an unmapped land.

My Day Is Ending

Lord,
you have been with me all through this day,
stay with me now.
As the shadows lengthen into darkness
let the noisy world grow quiet,
let its feverish concerns be stilled,
its voices silenced.

Let me understand and accept that
this is the most I can do,
the most you expect of me.

I need ask for nothing,
I need seek nothing.
I need only keep my heart flung wide open.

I am a stranger in a strange and bewildering place.

There are no familiar landmarks here,
nothing that I can cling to but you.

You will have to take my hand.

Keep me in your embrace,
in the dark silence
of this night,
and in the day to come
keep my eyes and my heart open to what is Real.

Day Thirty

My Day Begins

This journey into the Real
has brought us to a life
marked by new states of consciousness,
by new emotional experiences.

It has brought us
to a life that is above all else,
larger and more intense
than anything we have ever known
or imagined.

It has brought us to a life
that is positive,
not as some—perhaps even ourselves—have imagined
and feared.
It is not smaller and narrower,
not abstract and dreamy.

Rather than closing down our souls,
our journey into the Real
has opened them wide.

For the first time
we are experiencing the full scope of life
lived within the Reality of God.
For the first time we know
what it is like
for our hearts to beat,

to work within
the rhythms of God.

Our new life,
our Real life
will not come cheaply.
It will cost much.
It will make demands
on our loyalty, on our trust,
and on our capacity for self-sacrifice.

But for the first time
we are fully alive,
our will, our heart, and our mind
have been stretched to their limits.

We have found what is Real.

All Through the Day

We are alive.

My Day Is Ending

Lord,
you have been with me all through this day,
stay with me now.
As the shadows lengthen into darkness
let the noisy world grow quiet,
let its feverish concerns be stilled,
its voices silenced.

For the first time
I am fully alive.
You have stretched
my will, my heart, and my mind
to their limits.

I know for the first time

what it means
to live with what is Real,
to live with you.

But you will have to hold on to me.
I know that my grip on the Real,
on you,
is so tenuous,
I could let go at any moment.

I need you to stay with me,
to remind me of what is Real.

I need you
to be there,
when I am not sure.

One Final Word

This book not has been written as a final word, but as a gateway to the spiritual wisdom of a specific teacher, a gateway opening on your own spiritual path.

You may decide that Evelyn Underhill is someone whose experience of God is one that you wish to follow more closely and deeply. If so a wide variety of books is available. Over a lifetime she published many books that demonstrate a constantly growing mind and spirit. Still others are being developed from her notes and retreats. You might begin with *The Spiritual Life* or *Practical Mysticism*, both of which are widely available. Pray them as you have prayed this gateway book.

You may, on the other hand, decide that her experience and wisdom have not helped you. There are many other teachers. Somewhere there is the right teacher for your own, very special, absolutely unique journey of the spirit. You *will* find your teacher; you *will* discover your path. We would not be searching, as St. Augustine reminds us, if we had not already found.

One more thing should be said.

Spirituality is not meant to be self-absorption, a cocoon-like relationship between God and me. In the long run, if it is to have meaning, if it is to grow and deepen and not wither, it must be a wellspring of compassionate living. It must reach out to others as God has reached out to us. No one better captures this dimension of spirituality than Evelyn Underhill.

True spirituality, she repeatedly reminds us, breaks down the walls of our soul to let in not just heaven, but the whole world.

You May Want to Read

Evelyn Underhill: Modern Guide to the Ancient Quest for the Holy, edited with an introduction by Dana Greene. (State University of New York Press). The introduction to this collection of essays is an excellent short interpretive biography.

30-Days With a Great Spiritual Teacher Series

"The series is a treasure find for the busy person... this series is just enough to help the rushed executive as well as the harried parent find a quiet oasis in the midst of an overburdened schedule."
—Living Prayer

Titles in the 30-Days With a Great Spiritual Teacher Series:

LOVE WITHOUT MEASURE
The Spirituality of Mother Teresa

GRACE THROUGH SIMPLICITY
The Practical Spirituality of Evelyn Underhill

PEACE OF HEART
Life and Teachings of St. Francis of Assisi

SIMPLY SURRENDER
The Little Way of Thérèse of Lisieux

LET NOTHING DISTURB YOU
A Journey with Teresa Avila

FEAR NOT THE NIGHT
Classic Spirituality of John of the Cross

LET THERE BE LIGHT
The Visionary Spirituality of Hildegard of Bingen

LIVING IN THE PRESENCE OF GOD
The Everyday Spirituality of Brother Lawrence

YOU SHALL NOT WANT
A Spiritual Journey Based on The Psalms

THAT YOU MAY HAVE LIFE
Let The Mystics be Your Guide for Lent

WHERE ONLY LOVE CAN GO
Journey of the Soul into the Cloud of Unknowing

GOD AWAITS YOU
Based on the Classic Spirituality of Meister Eckhart

SET ASIDE EVERY FEAR
The Spirituality of Catherine of Siena

ALL WILL BE WELL
Based on the Classic Spirituality of Julian of Norwich

TRUE SERENITY
Based on Thomas á Kempis' The Imitation of Christ

SET YOUR HEART FREE
The Practical Spirituality of Francis de Sales

Prices and availability subject to change. Available at your local bookstore, online retailers, and from AVE MARIA PRESS at www.avemariapress.com or 1-800-282-1865